Words Of God

*A compilation of Prayers and Tablets
from the Bahá'í Writings*

Compiled at

The Bahá'í World Centre 1981

Immerse yourselves in the ocean of My words,
that ye may unravel its secrets, and
discover all the pearls of wisdom
that lie hid in its depths.

— Bahá'u'lláh

Words Of God

A compilation of Prayers and Tablets
from the Bahá'í Writings

Bahá'í
Publications
Australia

ISBN 0 90991 44 8

First printing B.E. 146 (1989)
Second edition 2005

Published by
Bahá'í Publications Australia

Distributed by
Bahá'í Distribution Services
P.O. Box 300
Bundoora Vic. 3083
Australia

Email address: bds@bahai.org.au

Website: www.bahaibooks.com

CONTENTS

Prayers

Selections from;

OBLIGATORY PRAYER*

I bear witness, O my God, that Thou hast created me to know Thee and to worship Thee. I testify, at this moment, to my powerlessness and to Thy might, to my poverty and to Thy wealth.

There is none other God but Thee, the Help in Peril, the Self-Subsisting.

— *Bahá'u'lláh*

*(Bahá'u'lláh revealed three obligatory prayers, one of which is to be chosen by each believer and recited by him once every 24 hours, in accordance with specific directions for each prayer. The instruction related to the prayer reproduced above, which is the shortest of the three, is that it must be recited once a day between noon and sunset.)

DAWN

O my God and my Master! I am Thy servant and the son of Thy servant. I have risen from my couch at this dawn-tide when the Day-Star of Thy oneness hath shone forth from the Day-Spring of Thy will, and hath shed its radiance upon the whole world, according to what had been ordained in the Books of Thy Decree.

Praise be unto Thee, O my God, that we have wakened to the splendors of the light of Thy knowledge. Send down, then, upon us, O my Lord, what will enable us to dispense with any one but Thee, and will rid us of all attachment to aught except Thyself. Write down, moreover, for me, and for such as are dear to me, and for my kindred, man and woman alike, the good of this world and the world to come. Keep us safe, then, through Thine unfailing protection, O Thou the Beloved of the entire creation and the Desire of the whole universe, from them whom Thou hast made to be the manifestations of the Evil Whisperer, who whisper in men's breasts. Potent art Thou to do Thy pleasure. Thou art, verily, the Almighty, the Help in Peril, the Self-Subsisting.

Bless Thou, O Lord my God, Him Whom Thou hast set over Thy most excellent titles, and through Whom Thou hast divided between the godly and the wicked, and graciously aid us to do what Thou lovest and desirest. Bless Thou, moreover, O my God, them Who are Thy Words and Thy Letters, and them who have set their faces towards Thee, and turned unto Thy face, and hearkened to Thy Call.

Thou art, truly, the Lord and King of all men, and art potent over all things.

— *Bahá'u'lláh*

MORNING

I have wakened in Thy shelter, O my God, and it becometh him that seeketh that shelter to abide within the Sanctuary of Thy protection and the Stronghold of Thy defense. Illumine my inner being, O my Lord, with the splendors of the Day-Spring of Thy Revelation, even as Thou didst illumine my outer being with the morning light of Thy favor.

— *Bahá'u'lláh*

I have risen this morning by Thy grace, O my God, and left my home trusting wholly in Thee, and committing myself to Thy care. Send down, then, upon me, out of the heaven of Thy mercy, a blessing from Thy side, and enable me to return home in safety even as Thou didst enable me to set out under Thy protection with my thoughts fixed steadfastly upon Thee.

There is none other God but Thee, the One, the Incomparable, the All-Knowing, the All-Wise.

— *Bahá'u'lláh*

EVENING

O my God, my Master, the Goal of my desire! This, Thy servant, seeketh to sleep in the shelter of Thy mercy, and to repose beneath the canopy of Thy grace, imploring Thy care and Thy protection.

I beg of Thee, O my Lord, by Thine eye that sleepeth not, to guard mine eyes from beholding aught beside Thee. Strengthen, then, their vision that they may discern Thy signs, and behold the Horizon of Thy Revelation. Thou art He before the revelations of Whose omnipotence the quintessence of power hath trembled.

No God is there but Thee, the Almighty, the All-Subduing, the Unconditioned.

— *Bahá'u'lláh*

THE FAST

Praise be to Thee, O Lord my God! I beseech Thee by this Revelation whereby darkness hath been turned into light, through which the Frequented Fane hath been built, and the Written Tablet revealed, and the Outspread Roll uncovered, to send down upon me and upon them who are in my company that which will enable us to soar into the heavens of Thy transcendent glory, and will wash us from the stain of such doubts as have hindered the suspicious from entering into the tabernacle of Thy unity.

I am the one, O my Lord, who hath held fast the cord of Thy loving-kindness, and clung to the hem of Thy mercy and favors. Do Thou ordain for me and for my loved ones the good of this world and of the world to come. Supply them, then, with the Hidden Gift Thou didst ordain for the choicest among Thy creatures.

These are, O my Lord, the days in which Thou hast bidden Thy servants to observe the fast. Blessed is he that observeth the fast wholly for Thy sake and with absolute detachment from all things except Thee. Assist me and assist them, O my Lord, to obey Thee and to keep Thy precepts. Thou, verily, hast power to do what Thou choosest.

There is no God but Thee, the All-Knowing, the All-Wise. All praise be to God, the Lord of all worlds.

— *Bahá'u'lláh*

MARRIAGE

Glory be unto Thee, O my God! Verily, this Thy servant and this Thy maid-servant have gathered under the shadow of Thy mercy and they are united through Thy favor and generosity. O Lord! Assist them in this Thy world and Thy Kingdom and destine for them every good through Thy bounty and grace. O Lord! Confirm them in Thy servitude and assist them in Thy service. Suffer them to become the signs of Thy Name in Thy world and protect them through Thy bestowals which are inexhaustible in this world and the world to come. O Lord! They are supplicating toward the Kingdom of Thy mercifulness and invoking toward the realm of Thy singleness. Verily, they are married in obedience to Thy command. Cause them to become the signs of harmony and unity until the end of time. Verily, Thou art Omnipotent, the Omnipresent and the Almighty!

— 'Abdu'l-Bahá

HEALING

Thy name is my healing, O my God, and remembrance of Thee is my remedy. Nearness to Thee is my hope, and love for Thee is my companion. Thy mercy to me is my healing and my succor in both this world and the world to come. Thou, verily, art the All-Bountiful, the All-Knowing, the All-Wise.

– Bahá'u'lláh

SPIRITUAL ASSEMBLY

Whenever ye enter the council chamber, recite this prayer with a heart throbbing with the love of God and a tongue purified from all but His remembrance, that the All-Powerful may graciously aid you to achieve supreme victory.

O God, my God! We are servants of Thine that have turned with devotion to Thy holy face, that have detached ourselves from all beside Thee in this glorious Day. We have gathered in this spiritual assembly, united in our views and thoughts, with our purposes harmonized to exalt Thy Word amidst mankind. O Lord, our God! Make us the signs of Thy divine guidance, the standards of Thy exalted Faith amongst men, servants to Thy mighty Covenant, O Thou our Lord Most High, manifestations of Thy Divine Unity in Thine Abhá Kingdom, and resplendent stars shining upon all regions. Lord! Aid us to become seas surging with the billows of Thy wondrous grace, streams flowing from Thine all-glorious heights, goodly fruits upon the tree of Thy heavenly Cause, trees waving through the breezes of Thy bounty in Thy celestial vineyard. O God! Make our souls dependent upon the verses of Thy Divine Unity, our hearts cheered with the outpourings of Thy grace, that we may unite even as the waves of one sea and become merged together as the rays of Thine effulgent light; that our thoughts, our views, our feelings may become as one reality, manifesting the spirit of union throughout the world. Thou art the Gracious, the Bountiful, the Bestower, the Almighty, the Merciful, the Compassionate.

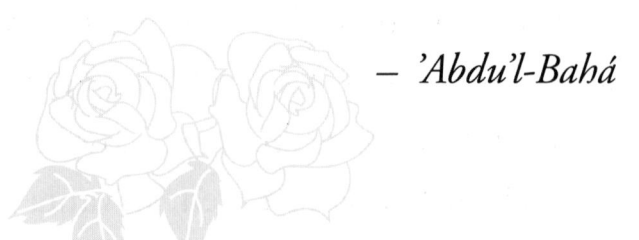

— *'Abdu'l-Bahá*

PRAYERS FOR CHILDREN AND YOUTH

O God! Rear this little babe in the bosom of Thy love, and give it milk from the breast of Thy Providence. Cultivate this fresh plant in the rose-garden of Thy love and aid it to grow through the showers of Thy bounty. Make it a child of the Kingdom, and lead it to Thy heavenly realm. Thou art powerful and kind, and Thou art the Bestower, the Generous, the Lord of surpassing bounty.

— *'Abdu'l-Bahá*

O God! Educate these children. These children are the plants of Thine orchard, the flowers of Thy meadow, the roses of Thy garden. Let Thy rain fall upon them; let the Sun of Reality shine upon them with Thy love. Let Thy breeze refresh them in order that they may be trained, grow and develop, and appear in the utmost beauty. Thou art the Giver. Thou art the Compassionate.

— *'Abdu'l-Bahá*

O Lord! Make this youth radiant, and confer Thy bounty upon this poor creature. Bestow upon him knowledge, grant him added strength at the break of every morn and guard him within the shelter of Thy protection so that he may be freed from error, may devote himself to the service of Thy Cause, may guide the wayward, lead the hapless, free the captives and awaken the heedless, that all may be blessed with Thy remembrance and praise. Thou art the Mighty and the Powerful.

— *'Abdu'l-Bahá*

O God, guide me, protect me, make of me a shining lamp and a brilliant star. Thou art the Mighty and the Powerful.

— *'Abdu'l-Bahá*

CONTRIBUTIONS TO THE FUND

All the friends of God ... should contribute to the extent possible, however modest their offering may be. God doth not burden a soul beyond its capacity. Such contributions must come from all centres and all believers. ... O Friends of God! Be ye assured that in place of these contributions, your agriculture, your industry, and your commerce will be blessed by manifold increases, with goodly gifts and bestowals. He who cometh with one goodly deed will receive a tenfold reward. There is no doubt that the living Lord will abundantly confirm those who expend their wealth in His path.

O God, my God! Illumine the brows of Thy true lovers, and support them with angelic hosts of certain triumph. Set firm their feet on Thy straight path, and out of Thine ancient bounty open before them the portals of Thy blessings; for they are expending on Thy pathway what Thou hast bestowed upon them, safeguarding Thy Faith, putting their trust in their remembrance of Thee, offering up their hearts for love of Thee, and withholding not what they possess in adoration for

Thy Beauty and in their search for ways to please Thee.

O my Lord! Ordain for them a plenteous share, a destined recompense and sure reward.

Verily, Thou art the Sustainer, the Helper, the Generous, the Bountiful, the Ever-Bestowing.

— *'Abdu'l-Bahá*

FOR THE DEPARTED

O my God! This is Thy servant and the son of Thy servant who hath believed in Thee and in Thy signs, and set his face towards Thee, wholly detached from all except Thee. Thou art, verily, of those who show mercy the most merciful.

Deal with him, O Thou Who forgivest the sins of men and concealest their faults, as beseemeth the heaven of Thy bounty and the ocean of Thy grace. Grant him admission within the precincts of Thy transcendent mercy that was before the foundation of earth and heaven. There is no God but Thee, the Ever-Forgiving, the Most Generous.

Let him, then, repeat six times the greeting "Alláh-u-Abhá," and then repeat nineteen times each of the following verses:

We all, verily, worship God.

We all, verily, bow down before God.

We all, verily, are devoted unto God.

We all, verily, give praise unto God.

We all, verily, yield thanks unto God.

We all, verily, are patient in God.

(If the dead be a woman, let him say: This is Thy handmaiden and the daughter of Thy handmaiden, etc. ...)

— Bahá'u'lláh

O my God! O Thou forgiver of sins, bestower of gifts, dispeller of afflictions!

Verily, I beseech Thee to forgive the sins of such as have abandoned the physical garment and have ascended to the spiritual world.

O my Lord! Purify them from trespasses, dispel their sorrows, and change their darkness into light. Cause them to enter the garden of happiness, cleanse them with the most pure water, and grant them to behold Thy splendors on the loftiest mount.

— 'Abdu'l-Bahá

♂OME OTHER PRAYERS

Glory be to Thee, O God, for Thy manifestation of love to mankind! O Thou Who art our Life and Light, guide Thy servants in Thy way, and make us rich in Thee and free from all save Thee.

O God, teach us Thy Oneness, and give us a realization of Thy Unity; that we may see no one save Thee. Thou art the Merciful and the Giver of bounty!

O God, create in the hearts of Thy beloved the fire of Thy love, that it may consume the thought of everything save Thee.

Reveal to us, O God, Thine exalted eternity - that Thou hast ever been and wilt ever be, and that there is no God save Thee. Verily, in Thee will we find comfort and strength!

– Bahá'u'lláh

O my God! O my God! Unite the hearts of Thy servants, and reveal to them Thy great purpose. May they follow Thy commandments and abide in Thy law. Help them, O God, in their endeavor, and grant them strength to serve Thee. O God, leave them not to themselves, but guide their steps by the light of Thy knowledge, and cheer their hearts by Thy love. Verily, Thou art their Helper and their Lord.

— *Bahá'u'lláh*

Say: O God, my God! Attire mine head with the crown of justice, and my temple with the ornament of equity. Thou, verily, art the Possessor of all gifts and bounties.

— *Bahá'u'lláh*

O my God! I ask Thee, by Thy most glorious Name, to aid me in that which will cause the affairs of Thy servants to prosper, and Thy cities to flourish. Thou, indeed, hast power over all things!

— *Bahá'u'lláh*

God grant that the light of unity may envelop the whole earth, and that the seal, "the Kingdom is God's", may be stamped upon the brow of all its peoples.

— *Bahá'u'lláh*

Is there any remover of difficulties save God? Say: Praised be God! He is God! All are His servants, and all abide by His bidding!

— *The Báb*

O God! Refresh and gladden my spirit. Purify my heart. Illumine my powers. I lay all my affairs in Thy hand. Thou art my Guide and my Refuge. I will no longer be sorrowful and grieved; I will be a happy and joyful being. O God! I will no longer be full of anxiety, nor will I let trouble harass me. I will not dwell on the unpleasant things of life.

O God! Thou art more friend to me than I am to myself. I dedicate myself to Thee, O Lord.

– 'Abdu'l-Bahá

O my Lord, my Beloved, my Desire! Befriend me in my loneliness and accompany me in my exile. Remove my sorrow. Cause me to be devoted to Thy beauty. Withdraw me from all else save Thee. Attract me through Thy fragrances of holiness. Cause me to be associated in Thy Kingdom with those who are severed from all else save Thee, who long to serve Thy sacred Threshold and who stand to work in Thy Cause. Enable me to be one of Thy maid-servants who have attained to Thy good pleasure. Verily, Thou art the Gracious, the Generous!

— 'Abdu'l-Bahá

O Lord my God! Assist Thy loved ones to be firm in Thy Faith, to walk in Thy ways, to be steadfast in Thy Cause. Give them Thy grace to withstand the onslaught of self and passion, to follow the light of divine guidance. Thou art the Powerful, the Gracious, the Self-Subsisting, the Bestower, the Compassionate, the Almighty, the All-Bountiful.

— *'Abdu'l-Bahá*

Lord! Pitiful are we, grant us Thy favor; poor, bestow upon us a share from the ocean of Thy wealth; needy, do Thou satisfy us; abased, give us Thy glory. The fowls of the air and the beasts of the field receive their meat each day from Thee, and all beings partake of Thy care and loving-kindness.

Deprive not this feeble one of Thy wondrous grace and vouchsafe by Thy might unto this helpless soul Thy bounty.

Give us our daily bread, and grant Thy increase in the necessities of life, that we may be dependent on none other than Thee, may commune wholly with Thee, may walk in Thy ways and declare Thy mysteries. Thou art the Almighty and the Loving and the Provider of all mankind.

— *’Abdu’l-Bahá*

O Lord! We are weak; strengthen us. O God! We are ignorant; make us knowing. O Lord! We are poor; make us wealthy. O God! We are dead; quicken us. O Lord! We are humiliation itself; glorify us in Thy Kingdom. If Thou dost assist us, O Lord, we shall become as scintillating stars. If Thou dost not assist us, we shall become lower than the earth. O Lord! Strengthen us. O God! Confer victory upon us. O God! Enable us to conquer self and overcome desire. O Lord! Deliver us from the bondage of the material world. O Lord! Quicken us through the breath of the Holy Spirit in order that we may arise to serve Thee, engage in worshiping Thee, and exert ourselves in Thy kingdom with the utmost sincerity. O Lord, Thou art Powerful. O God, Thou art Forgiving. O Lord, Thou art Compassionate.

— Abdu'l-Bahá

O God, my God! Shield Thy trusted servants from the evils of self and passion, protect them with the watchful eye of Thy loving-kindness from all rancor, hate and envy, shelter them in the impregnable stronghold of Thy care and, safe from the darts of doubtfulness, make them the manifestations of Thy glorious signs, illumine their faces with the effulgent rays shed from the Dayspring of Thy divine unity, gladden their hearts with the verses revealed from Thy holy kingdom, strengthen their loins by Thine all-swaying power that cometh from Thy realm of glory. Thou art the All-Bountiful, the Protector, the Almighty, the Gracious.

— *'Abdu'l-Bahá*

O God! O God! This is a broken-winged bird and his flight is very slow – assist him so that he may fly toward the apex of prosperity and salvation, wing his way with the utmost joy and happiness throughout the illimitable space, raise his melody in Thy Supreme Name in all regions, exhilarate the ears with this call, and brighten the eyes by beholding the signs of guidance.

O Lord! I am single, alone and lowly. For me there is no support save Thee, no helper except Thee and no sustainer beside Thee. Confirm me in Thy service, assist me with the cohorts of Thy angels, make me victorious in the promotion of Thy Word and suffer me to speak out Thy wisdom amongst Thy creatures. Verily, Thou art the helper of the weak and the defender of the little ones, and verily, Thou art the Powerful, the Mighty and the Unconstrained.

— *'Abdu'l-Bahá*

SELECTIONS FROM
*T*HE HIDDEN WORDS OF
BAHÁ'U'LLÁH

O SON OF BEING!

Thy Paradise is My love; thy heavenly home, reunion with Me. Enter therein and tarry not. This is that which hath been destined for thee in Our kingdom above and Our exalted dominion.

O SON OF SPIRIT!

Ask not of Me that which We desire not for thee, then be content with what We have ordained for thy sake, for this is that which profiteth thee, if therewith thou dost content thyself.

O SON OF MAN!

Breathe not the sins of others so long as thou art thyself a sinner. Shouldst thou transgress this command, accursed wouldst thou be, and to this I bear witness.

O SON OF MAN!

Deny not My servant should he ask anything from thee, for his face is My face; be then abashed before Me.

O SON OF BEING!

Bring thyself to account each day ere thou art summoned to a reckoning; for death, unheralded, shall come upon thee and thou shalt be called to give account for thy deeds.

O SON OF THE SUPREME!

I have made death a messenger of joy to thee. Wherefore dost thou grieve? I made the light to shed on thee its splendor. Why dost thou veil thyself therefrom?

O SON OF SPIRIT!

With the joyful tidings of light I hail thee: rejoice! To the court of holiness I summon thee; abide therein that thou mayest live in peace for evermore.

O SON OF MAN!

Neglect not My commandments if thou lovest My beauty, and forget not My counsels if thou wouldst attain My good pleasure.

O SON OF MAN!

Should prosperity befall thee, rejoice not, and should abasement come upon thee, grieve not, for both shall pass away and be no more.

O SON OF BEING!

If poverty overtake thee, be not sad; for in time the Lord of wealth shall visit thee. Fear not abasement, for glory shall one day rest on thee.

O SON OF BEING!

Busy not thyself with this world, for with fire We test the gold, and with gold We test Our servants.

O SON OF BEING!

Thy heart is My home; sanctify it for My descent. Thy spirit is My place of revelation; cleanse it for My manifestation.

O FRIEND!

In the garden of thy heart plant naught but the rose of love, and from the nightingale of affection and desire loosen not thy hold. Treasure the companionship of the righteous and eschew all fellowship with the ungodly.

O SON OF DUST!

Blind thine eyes, that thou mayest behold My beauty; stop thine ears, that thou mayest hearken unto the sweet melody of My voice; empty thyself of all learning, that thou mayest partake of My knowledge; and sanctify thyself from riches, that thou mayest obtain a lasting share from the ocean of My eternal wealth. Blind thine eyes, that is, to all save My beauty; stop thine ears to all save My word; empty thyself of all learning save the knowledge of Me; that with a clear vision, a pure heart and an attentive ear thou mayest enter the court of My holiness.

O MOVING FORM OF DUST!

I desire communion with thee, but thou wouldst put no trust in Me. The sword of thy rebellion hath felled the tree of thy hope. At all times I am near unto thee, but thou art ever far from Me. Imperishable glory I have chosen for thee, yet boundless shame thou hast chosen for thyself. While there is yet time, return, and lose not thy chance.

O SON OF EARTH!

Wouldst thou have Me, seek none other than Me; and wouldst thou gaze upon My beauty, close thine eyes to the world and all that is therein; for My will and the will of another than Me, even as fire and water, cannot dwell together in one heart.

O BEFRIENDED STRANGER!

The candle of thine heart is lighted by the hand of My power, quench it not with the contrary winds of self and passion. The healer of all thine ills is remembrance of Me, forget it not. Make My love thy treasure and cherish it even as thy very sight and life.

O YE RICH ONES ON EARTH!

The poor in your midst are My trust; guard ye My trust, and be not intent only on your own ease.

O SON OF PASSION!

Cleanse thyself from the defilement of riches and in perfect peace advance into the realm of poverty; that from the well-spring of detachment thou mayest quaff the wine of immortal life.

O SON OF MY HANDMAID!

Quaff from the tongue of the merciful the stream of divine mystery, and behold from the day-spring of divine utterance the unveiled splendor of the day-star of wisdom. Sow the seeds of My divine wisdom in the pure soil of the heart, and water them with the waters of certitude, that the hyacinths of knowledge and wisdom may spring up fresh and green from the holy city of the heart.

SELECTIONS FROM SOME
*T*ABLETS OF
BAHÁ'U'LLÁH

Verily I say, this is the Day in which mankind can behold the Face, and hear the Voice, of the Promised One. The Call of God hath been raised, and the light of His countenance hath been lifted up upon men. It behoveth every man to blot out the trace of every idle word from the tablet of his heart, and to gaze, with an open and unbiased mind, on the signs of His Revelation, the proofs of His Mission, and the tokens of His glory.

O ye children of men! The fundamental purpose animating the Faith of God and His Religion is to safeguard the interests and promote the unity of the human race, and to foster the spirit of love and fellowship amongst men. Suffer it not to become a source of dissension and discord, of hate and enmity. This is the straight Path, the fixed and immovable foundation. Whatsoever is raised on this foundation, the changes and chances of the world can never impair its strength, nor will the revolution of countless centuries undermine its structure

Immerse yourselves in the ocean of My words, that ye may unravel its secrets, and discover all the pearls of wisdom that lie hid in its depths. Take heed that ye do not vacillate in your determination to embrace the truth of this Cause — a Cause through which the potentialities of the might of God have been revealed, and His sovereignty established. With faces beaming with joy, hasten ye unto Him. This is the changeless Faith of God, eternal in the past, eternal in the future. Let him that seeketh, attain it; and as to him that hath refused to seek it - verily, God is Self-Sufficient, above any need of His creatures.

Say: This is the infallible Balance which the Hand of God is holding, in which all who are in the heavens and all who are on the earth are weighed, and their fate determined, if ye be of them that believe and recognize this truth. Say: Through it the poor have been enriched, the learned enlightened, and the seekers enabled to ascend unto the presence of God. Beware, lest ye make it a cause of dissension amongst you. Be ye as firmly settled as the immovable mountain in the Cause of your Lord, the Mighty, the Loving.

Be generous in prosperity, and thankful in adversity. Be worthy of the trust of thy neighbor, and look upon him with a bright and friendly face. Be a treasure to the poor, an admonisher to the rich, an answerer to the cry of the needy, a preserver of the sanctity of thy pledge. Be fair in thy judgment, and guarded in thy speech. Be unjust to no man, and show all meekness to all men. Be as a lamp unto them that walk in darkness, a joy to the sorrowful, a sea for the thirsty, a haven for the distressed, an upholder and defender of the victim of oppression. Let integrity and uprightness distinguish all thine acts. Be a home for the stranger, a balm to the suffering, a tower of strength for the fugitive. Be eyes to the blind, and a guiding light unto the feet of the erring. Be an ornament to the countenance of truth, a crown to the brow of fidelity, a pillar of the temple of righteousness, a breath of life to the body of mankind, an ensign of the hosts of justice, a luminary above the horizon of virtue, a dew to the soil of the human heart, an ark on the ocean of knowledge, a sun in the heaven of bounty, a gem on the diadem of wisdom, a shining light in the firmament of thy generation, a fruit upon the tree of humility.

The Ancient Beauty hath consented to be bound with chains that mankind may be released from its bondage, and hath accepted to be made a prisoner within this most mighty Stronghold that the whole world may attain unto true liberty. He hath drained to its dregs the cup of sorrow, that all the peoples of the earth may attain unto abiding joy, and be filled with gladness. This is of the mercy of your Lord, the Compassionate, the Most Merciful. We have accepted to be abased, O believers in the Unity of God, that ye may be exalted, and have suffered manifold afflictions, that ye might prosper and flourish. He Who hath come to build anew the whole world, behold, how they that have joined partners with God have forced Him to dwell within the most desolate of cities!

FROM *T*HE WRITINGS OF 'ABDU'L-BAHÁ

O thou who art turning thy face towards God! Close thine eyes to all things else, and open them to the realm of the All-Glorious. Ask whatsoever thou wishest of Him alone; seek whatsoever thou seekest from Him alone. With a look He granteth a hundred thousand hopes, with a glance He healeth a hundred thousand incurable ills, with a glimpse He layeth balm on every wound, with a nod He freeth the hearts from the shackles of grief. He doeth as He doeth, and what recourse have we? He carrieth out His Will, He ordaineth what He pleaseth. Then better for thee to bow down thy head in submission, and put thy trust in the All-Merciful Lord.